searching for blue sea glass

searching for blue sea glass

roger stevens

Rabbit Press

ISBN 0 9526541 1 3

First Published 2001 by
RABBIT PRESS
17 Martello Mews
Martello Road
Seaford
East Sussex
BN25 1JT

Printed in Great Britain by Biddles Ltd of Guildford, Surrey.

Book design by Joe Decie

This book is dedicated
To she who knows me best
Who operates my life's oasis
Who loves me on a daily basis
And will be forever blessed

Jill

Contents

Special Abilities
(Which might be useful)

Being able to determine
the moment when oven chips
are cooked just right.
To know how far there is to fall
from any height.

To always find (first time)
the trip switch
when the lights have fused.
To understand the feelings
of a friend
who stands confused.

In busy restaurants
(as everybody's leaving)
being able to sort out the coats.
Having perfect timing when recounting jokes
or anecdotes.

When planning picnics knowing
if it's going to rain.
The knack of rescuing a bee
trapped on the window pane.

To know which racehorse
is going to be a winner
and which will be a flop.
To gauge an audience reaction
when reading out a poem
and knowing when to stop.

(or keep going)

The Small Print

Where is Life's small print to be found?
Upon the midwife's fingernail?
Inscribed beneath the coffin lid
Below the winter ground?

Encoded in the entrails of a sacrifice?
Or in the way that green sea glass beads lie?
Perhaps it's hidden in the vapour trails
That decorate a summer's sky.

The Autumn Catalogue

Imagine if our clothes
Were living things
And in the autumn they withered
Green pullovers turning yellow, dying
Blue jeans turning purple, dead
Turn-ups curl-ups
Denim peeling away
Everywhere you look
People losing their clothes
Streets littered with remnants
Small brown snagged squares of tights
Scraps of socks
And everyone nude for the winter

Fat men with acres of previously hidden flesh
Wobbling along the wet pavements
Old thin women
Wrinkled and wafery
Huddled in Lowry groups
Like sticks blown into a corner

And naked through howling
Icy winds and squalls
Of snow everyone struggles gamely on
Until the spring
When clothes start growing again

Autobiography
(after Ferlinghetti)

I am leading
An exciting life
In my architect-designed
Luxury town house
Everyday I watch TV
The widescreen Nicam stereo
Takes my breath away
There are only two Soaps worth watching
Gameshows are going downhill
Mostly I am watching
24 hour News on
Sky Digital

I am leading
An exciting life
In my architect-designed
Appreciating town house
I have muesli for breakfast
I mix it myself
With the best organic ingredients
From Sainsbury's
Where I always shop
I have their loyalty card
Which I use to accumulate
Air Miles
And in the summer
I go to Spain
But off the beaten track
Along semi-deserted beaches
Where I contemplate upon
The vastness of the ocean

I am leading
An exciting life
In my architect-designed
Sought after town house
Everyday
I collect my e-mail
From the four corners of the world
And I e-respond
To a wide variety of people
Of many races
Whom I have made my friends
And they tell me colourful stories of riots
And the death squads
And the innocent in concrete cells
And the poor and ragged who cry on the streets
And send me their photos
And I send them mine
Which I scan on my Easy-3 scanner
At a resolution of 200 rpm

I am leading
An exciting life

Happy

A double-first degree
A lottery win
And a proposal of marriage
From an articulate, caring, sharing,
Intelligent and exceptionally
Beautiful Vogue model
Made Larry a very happy man.

Well,
When I'm with you
That's how happy I am

The Wrong Direction

Sitting on the train
Heading for home
Is a time for introspection
Although I'll be glad
To arrive
Unfortunately
You are in a hotel
In the other direction

Blue Shawl

The electric train pulls in
To the deserted station
And its echo rolls
Along the concrete platform

Then I spot
An old couple,
Well-wrapped
In a bright-blue shawl,
Huddled on a bench
Peering at a notebook.

Balloon

I filled a balloon
with thoughts of you
blown in with every puff
Into the blue
I let it go
and watched it soar
and sure enough
it burst and sent my love like rain
upon the world below

Hold On Tight

Hold on tight
when the razor-toothed dinosaurs
of doubt disturb the night
and the vorpal-bladed jabberwock
of worry wants to fight
and the flighty phantom flitter-mouse
of fear rears up to bite -
hold on tight.

Turn on the light
and the parade
of monsters that you made
will fade.
And one last thing -
you know
that if your
worst scenario
should try to lay you low
then I'll be there to catch you
when you let go.

Access All Areas

You wore a tag
Around your neck
It said

Mad person
In love
May be found
Wandering,
Apparently aimlessly,
In restricted areas
Of the heart
And the mind

Please
Make allowances

Jools Holland
Dec 96

you held my arm
an intimate moment
in a vast sea of music
as the jazz hit the rocks

and sprayed us all
with boogie woogie

Hank Marvin

Thank you, Hank
For your Wonderful Land
Bert Weedon was not a patch on you

But now, I'm afraid,
You are a Shadow of your former self

Elvis Has Just Left The Bathroom

Elvis has just left the bathroom
In a terrible mess
There are greasy hairs in the comb
Barbiturates in the basin &
Rhinestones scattered over the floor
Like confetti

Prior
To joining the Angelic Choir
Many regarded him as
A fat old git
But when he was young
He set the world on fire
Singing

Hound Dog
And Heartbreak Hotel

Uh uh uh
Uh uh uh
Uh uh uh
Oh yeah

Joan of Arc

Everyone thought it odd
that Joan of Arc heard voices

From God.

For being a witch and for foretelling that the
English would be defeated by the French and
thrown out of France
(except for Calais)
she was burned at the stake which,
in those less-civilised and deadly times,
is about what one might expect.
But as it turned out she was

Correct.

The Origin of the Clerihew

Edmund Clerihew Bentley's fame grew
When he invented the clerihew
But if he'd wanted a fortune
He would have been wise
To invent the double cheeseburger,
With fries.

(i read a poet who)

i read a poet who
always bracketed her titles

i read a poet who
Nearly always used lower case letters

i read a poet who
never used one rhyme when two would do

i read a poet who
was a word-dog
who herded words into a corner
and took them nowhere

i read a poet who
condemned the wind for being non-committal

i read a poet who
shouted from the roof tops
but nobody looked up

i read a poet who
was so serious he turned into a pillar of lead

i read a poet whose words tumbled from the page
like burnt peas from a pan

i read a poet who
was a million things but above all
was no poet

Through The Heart-shaped Window

I see you through the window of my love
I feel your warmth through the skylight of my need
I touch you through
the kitchen hatch of apprehension
I smell you through the grate of our bright fire
You confuse me through the wall of our illusions
As I stumble through the blinds, a wounded dove,
To understand you through the doors
of my perception
I kiss you through the keyhole of desire
I send you notes up the chimney to heaven above
I build upon the foundations of our Friendship
Only to slide down the roof tiles of your deception
And to be taken away
in the giant skip of poetry that's dire

Delivery Expected Later

Sorry, the shopkeeper said
We're fresh out of similes today
Like a ... er...
Or like... um...
Anyway, come back later
We're expecting a new batch in

Although
I've some
Amazing and audacious alliteration
If you're interested

Support Your Local Poet

I like to think
That when I buy a book of poems
I'm buying the poet a loaf of bread

Your Kisses

Your kisses
Taste of
Lady Grey
Toothpaste
Laughter
Christmas Day
Of walking in the morning light
Half asleep and early nights
Happy-flavour chewing gum
Promises of fun to come
A million-billion well-chewed words
That leave your lips, wise and absurd
Holidays across the seas
Of secrets shared and memories
The songs of Caravan
The hums of honey-making bees
And sensual, subtle harmonies
Your kisses taste
Of all of these

Hiding

I find you hiding in the most
unexpected places, bridging my
past and my future with your
now

Our Universe

Aurora Borealis
Is a long, long road to run
But with you beside me
We can travel to the sun
And as we go we'll circumvent
The Universe of stars
We'll ride the fabled chariot
And hang a left by Mars
And as the stars, like silver fruit,
Ripen before our eyes
We'll pick them as the moons
Of Jupiter begin to rise
In our silver spaceship
Watch the dawning of creation
As we soar like supernovas
Of our cosmic imagination

shall I compare thee to (a)

(a) the cool gold of morning
that creeps around the curtains
and lifts the shadows from your face
a sunny smile
a summer's day
the world in a grain of sand
a Scrabble board,
two blanks
Y U R A
rose
by any other

(b) thou art
more beautiful than (a)

The (alternative) Six Senses

1 warmth
emerging from the tangled wrack of sleep
you wake beside me

2 hope
when the sky's a mass of bruises
and the wind is rising
in the back of night's throat
a stray ray of sunlight
hits a gliding gull

3 danger
as we pick our way
through the highwater debris
of yesterday's dreams,
an empty rowing boat
bobs on the calm water

4 vision
I see us sprightly wise
receiving our trophy
for a century of contributions
to the loving arts

5 rightness
a minefield we successfully negotiate

6 destiny
when about to fall
from the cliff-top of adolescence
knowing that,
however long the drop,
you would one day be there to catch me

Holiday Treasures

A pebble (Sheerness)
A shell (Skegness)
A rash (Ibiza)
A bell (Tibet)
A postcard (unposted)
A letter (unwritten)
A promise (unkept)
A photo (kept hidden)

San Francisco Haiku
(excerpts from a longer poem)

there's a wind tonight
the fog drifts over the bay
Bob Dylan singing

SF MOMA hot
a cool black and white building
a feast for the eyes

whatever happened
to that long-ago summer
in Haight Ashbury?

the park after dark
a wash of sensuous sound
the golden city

fog over Frisco
there's art and jazz on Filmore
the Fourth of July

summertime and the
doo bi doo dah di doo dah
ba bi bi do dee

on Fisherman's Wharf
the world is on holiday
and caught in its nets

crabstalls and tee shirts
and a dollar for your thoughts
the dawn's greedy light

Fireworks

The Universe
Is a firework display
Filmed at
One frame a millennium

Number of Stars

If every star in this galaxy
Were a grain of salt
The grains would fill
An Olympic-sized swimming pool
And if the pool
Was filled with water
It would be
Very
Very
Salty

I like trees

Oh *Laburnum alpinum*
and *Laburnum anagyroides*
I think you're lovely
and you, too, *Aesculus*
with your oblong-elliptic leaflets
beautiful *Cytisus purpureus*
and nice *Acer griseum*
I love to lie beneath
a *Quercus pubescens*
chase around a *Morus nigra*
or a gorgeous *Myrica gale*
poor, sad *Salix aurita*
and popular *Populus trichocarpa*
pretty *Platanus orientalis*
and sagacious *Sambucus*
spruce *Picea omorika*
and dapper *Daphne mezereum*
I like you
from your roots
to your tips
because I like trees
from their blossom
to their hips

Insult

A notion currently inhabiting
My brain is that
The glands beneath your skin
That produce minute particles
Designed to be carried
By tiny airborne currents
And picked up by nerves
In the mucous membrane
Covering the upper turbinal bone
And the nasal septum
And triggering impulses
Along olfactory nerves
That pass through minute holes
In the cribriform plate
Of the ethmoid bone
Into the olfactory bulb
In the nose
And thus to the
Olfactory tract
In the brain
Are over producing
Again

Or to put it
Another way

I think
You stink!

Snail

Shell
Mantle
Eye
Tentacle
Mouth
Foot

What an uncomplicated creature
You are

vewol mevoments

vewel movemonts
vowel mevoments
vewol mevemonts
vowel movements

Party Line

I am in a room
At a party
When everyone's mobile phone rings
At the same time
The sound is appalling
I block up my ears with small sausages
In desperation I dive into the mousse
To drown
Where I wonder -
Is this how
Death By Chocolate
Was conceived?

How Father Got Further

My father
Worked in the prosthetics industry
Worked his way up
From ankles to necks
He was a self-made man

Changing Rooms

Cheer up, room
I'll draw a smile
On your wall

Oh dear,
It hasn't turned out
Quite the way I intended

Moving House

Moving house is very...
Well, it's...

Unfortunately
The word I am searching for
Is in a crate
In a warehouse
In Nottingham
With the rest of our
Worldly belongings

The Key to your Heart

The key to your heart
Is it iron?
Blackened, rusted, heavy,
Slow to turn
The lock's stiff mechanism
In the stone wall
Deep below ground?

The key to your heart
Is it silver?
Crafted by moonlight
A mystic design of intricate filigree
A mirror of the ancient craftsman's face
His deft fingertips awakening
In the smooth surface
Half-hidden memories of lovers

The key to your heart
Is it wooden?
Sleeping a winter's sleep
The wood wakes slowly as the sap
Begins to soften, move
The greenness encoded within
Is slowly released

No, the key to your heart
Is made of invisible materials
Formed by laughter
Shaped by love
Held by promises
Turned by smiles
In the lock of truth

Best Before

and by the way -
never leave it
past the tell-by date
to tell someone
you love them

best tell them every day
to be on the safe side

Night Adventures

in the darkness
we sleep
we dream
wrapped up
within our own worlds

but our bodies
touch, slide, interact
caressing
unselfconsciously

we stir
grasp the dream's tail
stumble half awake
into the freezing darkness
to empty our bladders
fetch a drink
let the dog out

and in the bed
upon the still warm sheets
we've left
the faint imprint
of lovers

Poised

between a deep breath
and a loving sigh

the future
hangs
expectantly

Consider the Silence

(after a trial - Indian jurors consider the quality of the silence itself for indications of truthfulness, deception, innocence or guilt.)

When the plumbing takes a breather
When the seagulls take a breath
When the visiting team scores
When we respect a death

When the fridge stops shaking
When we close our eyes and pray
When you asked that we be married
And I said
Okay

Casualty
(Summer 2000)

Saturday night
And the waiting room is an oven

We watch the little boy
With the bloody nose
Climb across the chairs

Dad with a towel to his head
To keep the bleeding to a minimum

Digital noticeboard flashes
Current waiting time of
Four to five hours

Well, the youth snarls into
The phone along the corridor,
He was fucking out of order
I didn't hit him
I just fucking pushed him away

Somewhere a baby is crying
A woman with an asthma attack
Is rushed through

The spots of blood
On the tired brown vinyl floor
Resemble the constellation
Florence the Nightingale

A nurse yells a name three times.
Too late, she grins. He'll have to miss
His turn.

Christ on the Water

the golden light settles like dust
on the hills of Galilee
in the purple shadows of hill and vine
the brittle snap of disturbed bleached bones
the clang of sword upon sword
the soft hack of metal cleaving flesh

on the wave's crest
the old salt flies above the cannon smoke
dances briefly, tumbles
dilutes the sea with blood

in the freezing mud
the soldier's teeth
chatter chaotic morse

in the backstreet rubble
a child digs blindly
for her mother
who only heard the whistle
not the explosion

in the achingly beautiful sky
a ragged black line
scratched by the smoking aeroplane

until the last tear falls in the burning rain
Christ on the water
walks in pain

the dipping pool

upon a spindly deckcrabchair
jabbing the wet cossie sea
glare at the automatic zimmer frames
and horoscope games
and sad shove-ha'penny
but, my love, gaze lovingly
into the dipping pool

surfing the grey foam
the traffic-jammed cut-glass
dog-scarred beach
where nightmare scarefair undertow torn
underwear worn weary caught unawares
and odd unpolluted nudists
peer happily, my love,
into the dipping pool

dream shrimping nets
and home-made tiddlers
seaweed cake and sunrise dazzlers
pier shows and windmills cricket skills
and the puzzle and guzzle of crazy golf
reflected, my love,
in the dipping pool

it slowly and inexorably dawns
on the fractured cling-filmed
taxi-dermied shoppers
hustling the faded arcades
fishbowl rifle-range clutter
you've tortured the inflatable dinosaur
cast adrift, my love,
in the dipping pool

TV Lover

I saw you in the adverts
And ordered you
On your special number

At last
You appeared in my life
And I loved you

I adjusted the widescreen control
(I never liked girls who were too thin)
Altered the level of colour
To bring out the blue
In your eyes
Tweaked the contrast
To lighten your hair
And darken your skin
Turned down the volume
And turned up the bass just a smidgeon
For those husky notes

My Girlfriend Guide informed me
You would be round every Saturday at 7
But if I missed you
You'd be round again on Sunday at 11
To be on the safe side
I set the video

Now your transmission is over
I often replay the bit
Where you said
You loved me too

The Tale of Edward and Lizzie

Edward moved with casual ease
Ideas tumbled with the breeze
Lizzie sat with tied constraint
Words pulled tight enough to faint

Edward called the clouds to tango
Melodies danced round his hands
Lizzie painted with precision
Dotted Ts and polished sand

It was obvious to the world
Watching from another place -
Lizzie struggling with a thimble
Ed demolishing a case -

That the pair were most unlikely
Lovers. They'd not travel far.
The world would watch their love unravel
Like a burnt-out shooting star

But Lizzie gave Edward direction
Focus - and a place to start.
Ed gave Lizzie fire and passion
Opened doors within her heart.

Now Edward studies microcosms
Know the secrets deep within
Lizzie lies beneath the stars
And kisses Edward on the chin

On Guard

Guard your early days with bayonets
Guard your youth with smoke and fire
Your daring deeds patrol with tanks
Your quest for truth hold with barbed wire

Protect your early days with tissue
Wrap them up in cotton wool
The memory of your first kiss
Holding hands after school

Or toss your past life on the bonfire
Abandon it, like firewood
Neglect it, kick it, disrespect it

Either way, it's gone for good

Reflection

Is it me?
Or is my reflection
Looking younger?

It's a surprise.
I seem to be growing
More youthful.

Is it me?
Or just my eyes?

Do You Talk About Me When I'm Gone?

When I walk out the door
Do you turn to your friends and say
He was a tall man
We will miss him
While he's at the shops

Do you say
Oh, how his remaining hair
Shone in the evening sun
His stoop was less pronounced today
Why, he was rarely out of breath

Do you say
Remember when
He made us laugh?

Do you say
He was kind
He was eager to please
Although not in a weak way

Do you say
Let us board the spaceship, Miranda
It's chilly here upon the verandah

Job Opportunities

I could have trained for the first man on Mars
Blur asked me to sort out their lights
I've turned down lucrative offers
To work on building sites
Richard Branson even begged me
Help him run some business sessions
I said, Look, Rich, Life *is* a bitch
But *Poet* is my chosen profession

I could be up (or down) at the crack of dawn
In a New York elevator
Or baking bread on a ship in the Med
But I prefer to rise much later
As you work in your factories, offices too,
You may *think* that life's hardships I shirk
But I wrestle with words
(and sit watching the birds)
Writing poems is bloody hard work

Award Ceremony

I stand on the stage in the spotlight
'Tho the spotlight isn't for me
I read from the envelope held in my hand
And now, in the category

Most Wonderful Woman in
All of the World...
(And the air could be scooped with a spoon)
The winner is... (open the envelope) ...YOU
And the cameras zoom round the room

'Til they pick you out, looking flustered,
Excited and pleased, all in one
You walk on to the stage to
Tremendous applause
You're the favourite with everyone

But while you're enjoying the spotlight
And cheers of the crowd ringing loud
I am standing quite quietly beside you
Feeling unbelievably proud

The Last Poem I Ever Wrote
(after Henry Normal)

I hope the last poem I ever wrote
Never gets written

When I'm Dead

When I'm dead my ghost will walk
The ramparts of Castle Regret
My ghost will sing
I remember Paris
My ghost will dance
In the vapour-trails of could-have-beens

When I'm dead my ghost will walk
The pathways of power
My ghost will laugh in the Oval Office
Cry in the Kremlin
Uncover deceits
Cut the blood-red tape that binds
Unholy alliances
Put the wind up presidents

When I'm dead my ghost
Will ride forth in a black chariot
With an army of stunted souls
To scare the shit out of crap teachers

When I'm dead
My ghost will follow you, my love,
Silently and secretly
And weave strands of joy into your dreams
Blow you kisses of contentment
Guard the door of your bedroom
And whisper everything's all right